LUXURY VACATION RENTALS

A Safe and Profitable Investment

LUXURY VACATION RENTALS

Copyright © 2023

PREFACE

In the world of luxury vacation rentals, success hinges on a delicate balance of art and science. It requires a keen understanding of the market, a passion for delivering exceptional guest experiences, and a commitment to safeguarding and enhancing property values. This book, "Luxury Vacation Rentals: A Safe and Profitable Investment", is the result of the collective expertise and dedication of three remarkable individuals: Patrick Poulin, Patrick Beland, and Stephanie Bessette.

Patrick Poulin, a developer, trainer, and coach specializing in vacation chalets and short-term rentals/Airbnb with Immofacile, is a testament to the power of creativity in the real estate market. His journey began as a chalet owner, but it was his expertise in creative financing and his appearances on a television program that elevated him to a league of his own. By the end of 2018, in collaboration with his business partner, Patrick Beland, he co-founded Reserver.ca, a property management company committed to meeting the needs of investors seeking to optimize their property calendars, protecting their assets, while offering flexibility. Patrick Poulin's recipe for success revolves around what he dubs the "triple WOW": the first impression, execution, and communication.

Patrick Beland, an expert in real estate prospecting and optimizing rental yields, stands as a beacon of insight for property investors. As both an esteemed investor and owner of short-term rental properties across the globe, his invaluable experience has been pivotal to the accomplishments of Reserver.ca. Clients have testified to the remarkable growth in rental income and profitability they have achieved under his guidance. With over 25 years of extensive experience in the technology sector, he brings a unique perspective to the company. Patrick is also developing an exclusive business intelligence application tailored to the short-term rental industry. This revolutionary tool can analyze and uncover the most lucrative locations in Quebec and around the world, enabling investors to pinpoint the best areas for investment.

Starting in 2017, both Patricks have been passionately collaborating to establish an all-encompassing project specifically focused on short-term rentals in the sought-after region of Sainte-Adèle. This groundbreaking initiative spans more than 70 available plots, strategically positioned to address the scarcity of vacation chalets close to Montreal. For further information, please visit airbnbinvestmentproperty.com.

Stephanie Besette, a seasoned professional with over two decades of experience in the customer service industry, has harnessed her passion for management to serve as

4

Reserver.ca's General Manager. Her role in ensuring seamless guest experiences and her active involvement in the company's development have earned her the trust and admiration of clients.

This book embodies their collective wisdom and the lessons learned from countless property owners who have sought to maximize their earnings, deliver unforgettable guest experiences, and protect and enhance their property assets. The reviews we've received from clients and partners speak volumes about the impact of our strategies and the dedication we bring to every endeavor.

Inside these pages, you will find a comprehensive guide that will help you navigate the intricacies of the luxury vacation rental market. From crafting compelling listings to leveraging automation for popularity management, from optimizing rental income to attracting high-paying, respectful guests, we have covered every aspect of your journey to success.

We believe in our ability to make a difference in the world of vacation rentals, and we want you to share in that success. To demonstrate our commitment, we offer you a FREE analysis of your property's rental potential. This personalized assessment will provide you with invaluable insights into how you can maximize your returns and elevate your luxury vacation rental business to new heights. Contact us at 1 (833) 335-2583 or partnerup@reserver.ca to elevate your rental business.

As you embark on this journey with us, we encourage you to absorb the knowledge within these pages, implement the strategies we share, and seize the opportunities that lie ahead. We are dedicated to your success, and we look forward to being a part of your journey toward achieving unparalleled success in the vacation rental market.

Welcome to a world of vacation property rentals, success, and unforgettable experiences.

The Authors and the Team at Reserver.ca

TABLE OF CONTENTS

INTRODUCTION:

THE LUXURY VACATION RENTAL MARKET

Welcome to the world of luxury vacation rental properties! As a luxury vacation property rental manager and owner, I have had the unique opportunity to experience the industry from both sides, and I am excited to share my knowledge and expertise with those who are looking to turn their luxury property into a profitable business.

The luxury vacation rental market has seen a significant growth in recent years, with more and more people choosing to invest in high-end properties as a way to generate income and create a profitable business. If you are someone who is fortunate enough to own a luxury property and are looking to share and profit from it while ensuring your property is well taken care of and accessible to you whenever you want, then this book is for you.

As a luxury vacation property rental manager, I have had the pleasure of working with some of the most beautiful and prestigious properties around the world. I have seen firsthand what it takes to create and manage a successful luxury vacation rental business. It takes knowledge, strategy, and dedication to create a successful and profitable business.

In this book, we will cover a wide range of topics, including how to define the property's unique selling points, research target market's demographics and travel preferences, market the property effectively, and create a first-class guest experience. We will also discuss the importance of building a strong reputation and maintaining positive reviews, as well as tips on how to increase occupancy and maximize revenue.

One of the most important aspect of creating a successful luxury vacation rental business is to attract only the best guests, receive 5 star reviews and maximize profitability, all while ensuring the property is well taken care of and accessible to the owner whenever they want. I will be teaching you how to identify your target market and how to appeal to their preferences and needs, how to create a memorable guest experience, and how to use marketing and promotion effectively.

You will learn about how to create an irresistible listing, how to price your property competitively, and how to use technology and automation to make managing your property more efficient. You will also learn about the importance of guest communication and providing a high-level of customer service, as well as tips for handling difficult situations and complaints.

We will also cover important legal and financial aspects of owning and renting out a luxury vacation property. This will include understanding tax implications, insurance requirements, and local regulations. Additionally, we will discuss how to set up a legal and transparent rental agreement, and how to handle any disputes or legal issues that may arise.

This book is designed for luxury property owners and aspiring luxury vacation property managers who are looking to turn their property into a profitable business. It is a comprehensive guide that covers all aspects of creating and managing a successful luxury vacation rental business. With the insights, strategies, and tips provided in this book, you will be able to create a successful and profitable business, while ensuring your property is well taken care of and accessible to you whenever you want.

In conclusion, running a luxury vacation rental property can be a great way to make money and enjoy your property at the same time. By understanding your target market and their preferences, and creating a memorable guest experience, you can attract the right guests and get 5-star reviews. You also need to make sure your property is well taken care of and accessible to you. With the right strategies and knowledge, you can create a successful and profitable luxury vacation rental business.

Little-known fact

A little-known fact about the luxury vacation rental market is that many high-end properties are now being used for events and special occasions, such as destination weddings, corporate retreats, and private parties. This trend is known as "event rentals" and it's becoming an increasingly popular way for luxury property owners to generate additional revenue and make the most of their property. Event rentals can provide an opportunity for property owners to earn higher rates, and also to attract a different type of clientele. This can increase the property's occupancy rate, and also provide a new revenue stream.

1.

IDENTIFYING AND ANALYZING THE TARGET MARKET

Defining the Property's Unique Selling Points

When it comes to your luxury vacation rental, it's important to remember that what makes your property special, sets it apart from the rest! It could be something as simple as a stunning ocean view, or a cozy fireplace, a luxurious spa or a private pool. Take some time to wander around your property and make a list of all the things that make it special and would make your guests feel welcome and excited to stay there.

Now that you have a list of all the unique and special aspects of your property, it's time to think about how you can show off these features to potential guests. For example, if your property has a beautiful garden, you can highlight that by taking some great photos and showcasing them in your property listing or on your website. You can also think about offering guests the chance to use the garden during their stay.

It's important to remember that not everyone will be interested in the same things when it comes to vacation rentals. That's why it's important to think about what types of guests your property will appeal to the most. For example, if your property is located in a bustling city, it may be a perfect fit for business travelers who need a comfortable place to stay while they're on the go. On the other hand, if your property is located in a secluded rural area, it may be ideal for couples or families looking for a peaceful getaway. By understanding your target guests and the unique selling points of your property, you'll be able to market it in a way that appeals to them.

By following these steps, you'll be able to create a marketing strategy that effectively showcases the property's best features and appeals to your target guests. And not just that, but you'll also be able to make sure that your guests are having a wonderful stay, and they'll be more likely to leave a great review and come back again!

Researching Target Market's Demographics

When it comes to attracting guests to your luxury vacation rental, understanding your target market's demographics is key. Demographics include things like age, income, family status, and occupation. By understanding these factors, you'll be able to tailor your marketing efforts to appeal to the specific group of people that are most likely to book a stay at your property.

The demographics of your target market can have a big impact on the type of guests that will be interested in your property.

For example, if you are targeting families, you may want to emphasize amenities such as a large backyard and a swimming pool. On the other hand, if you are targeting business travelers, you may want to emphasize amenities such as a home office and high-speed internet. Understanding how demographics impact the type of guests interested in your property will help you make informed decisions about the features and amenities you offer.

Once you have a good understanding of your target market's demographics, you can start tailoring your offering to appeal to that specific group of people. This may include things like offering special discounts to families or business travelers, or highlighting amenities that will appeal to your target market. For example, if you are targeting young professionals, you may want to offer high-speed internet and a workspace with a standing desk. Or if you are targeting retirees, you may want to offer a discounted rate for a longer stay, and to promote the peacefulness and proximity of your location.

By researching your target market's demographics and tailoring your offering accordingly, you'll be able to attract the type of guests that are most likely to enjoy and appreciate your property. This in turn will lead to happier guests and more positive reviews, ultimately leading to greater profitability.

Identifying Target Market's Travel Preferences

In addition to understanding your target market's demographics, it's also important to understand their travel preferences. This includes things like the type of vacation they are looking for, their preferred activities, and the type of accommodation they are looking for. By understanding your target market's travel preferences, you'll be able to tailor your marketing efforts to attract the guests that are the best fit for your property.

Once you have a good understanding of your target market's travel preferences, it's important to consider how they align with the property. For example, if your property is located in a bustling city, it may be well-suited to guests who are looking for an urban vacation experience. On the other hand, if your property is located in a secluded rural area, it may be better suited to guests looking for a more tranquil and peaceful getaway. By considering how your target market's travel preferences align with your property, you'll be able to create a more effective marketing strategy.

Once you have a good understanding of your target market's travel preferences and how they align with your property, you can start tailoring your offering to appeal to that specific group of people. This may include things like offering package deals for guests interested in outdoor activities, or highlighting the property's proximity to popular tourist attractions for guests looking for a more adventurous vacation experience. You can also think of offering a concierge service, or even personalize the stay for your guests. For example, if you know that your guests are foodies, you can offer to arrange for them to have a private chef or cooking class during their stay.

By researching and understanding your target market's travel preferences, and tailoring your offering accordingly, you'll be able to attract the type of guests that are most likely to enjoy and appreciate your property, leading to happier guests and more positive reviews, ultimately leading to greater profitability.

Summary

In conclusion, when it comes to luxury vacation rental properties, it's important to identify and analyze the target market. This means understanding who your potential guests are and what they are looking for in a vacation rental. By understanding your target market, you can make your property more appealing to them by highlighting the unique selling points of your property, the amenities and services it offers, and the local market conditions. This will help you attract the right guests, get good reviews, and make more money.

Little known fact

A little-known fact about identifying and analyzing the target market is that many luxury vacation rental properties target multiple market segments at the same time. This means that instead of only targeting one specific group of guests, the property owner will try to appeal to several different groups by offering a variety of amenities and services that cater to different interests. For example, a property located in a coastal area may offer not only beach amenities but also options for boating and fishing, or a property located in a city, may offer not only cultural experiences but also business amenities to cater to corporate travelers. By appealing to multiple market segments, the property owner can increase their bookings and revenue by reaching a larger audience.

Real life example

Let's say you own a luxury vacation rental in the wine country of Napa Valley, California. Some of the property's unique selling points include:

- The property has a large vineyard on the property, which allows guests to explore the vines and learn about winemaking.
- The property has a private chef on-site who can prepare gourmet meals for guests during their stay.
- The property has a swimming pool, a hot tub, and a sauna, which offer guests the opportunity to relax and unwind.

To market these unique selling points, you can highlight them in your property listing and on your website. For example, you can include photos of the vineyard on your listing and website, and emphasize the opportunity for guests to explore the vines and learn about winemaking. You can also highlight the private chef service, and offer package deals that include gourmet meals. Also, you can include pictures of the pool, hot tub and sauna, and emphasize the opportunity for guests to relax and unwind during their stay.

By highlighting these unique selling points, you'll be able to attract guests who are interested in experiencing the wine country, who are foodies or are looking for a relaxing getaway. Additionally, you can host wine tastings, vineyard tour, and wine making classes, which will allow the guest to experience the unique selling point of your property in a more interactive way.

In general, by highlighting the unique selling points of your property, you'll be able to attract the right guests and increase the chances of getting high-end bookings and 5-star reviews.

Here is another example
Let's say you own a luxury vacation rental on the coast of Costa Rica with a stunning ocean view. Some of the property's unique selling points include:

- The property has direct access to a secluded and private beach, which allows guests to enjoy the warm

tropical waters and white sandy beaches in a more secluded environment.

- The property has a fully equipped outdoor kitchen,
  which allows guests to enjoy al fresco dining while taking in the beautiful ocean views.
- The property has a rooftop terrace with a Jacuzzi,
  which offers guests the opportunity to relax and unwind
  while taking in the panoramic ocean views.

To market these unique selling points, you can highlight them
in your property listing and on your website. For example, you
can include photos of the private beach, and emphasize the
opportunity for guests to enjoy the beach in a secluded and
private environment. You can also highlight the outdoor
kitchen, and offer package deals that include a private chef to
prepare meals for guests. And you can also take some great
photos from the rooftop terrace and Jacuzzi, and emphasizing
the opportunity for guests to relax and unwind while taking in
the panoramic ocean views.

By highlighting these unique selling points, you'll be able to
attract guests who are looking for a private and secluded
beach vacation experience, who enjoy outdoor dining and appreciate a beautiful ocean view. Additionally, you can think
about offering some beach activities like surf or snorkel lessons, and include it as part of the package. Also, you can offer

a concierge service to book some tours of the local area, including local restaurants, and excursions like jungle hiking or mangrove kayak tours.

In general, by highlighting the unique selling points of your property, you'll be able to attract the right guests and increase the chances of getting high-end bookings and 5-star reviews. This way, guests will be able to experience the best of Costa Rica's tropical paradise, and enjoy a memorable vacation that offers the perfect balance of adventure, relaxation, and indulgence.

Here are example of descriptions we would create
Indulge in a one-of-a-kind wine country experience at our luxurious vineyard retreat in Napa Valley! Nestled in the heart of California's renowned wine region, our property offers a unique blend of elegance, tranquility, and adventure.

Picture yourself waking up to breathtaking views of the vines, right outside your window. As our guest, you'll have exclusive access to our private vineyard, where you can take a stroll, learn about winemaking, and taste some of the finest wines the region has to offer. Imagine sipping on a glass of delicious local wine while enjoying a picnic lunch amidst the grapes.

But that's not all, our property has more to offer! Our private chef will delight your taste buds with gourmet meals, tailored to your preferences, during your stay. Indulge in a romantic candlelit dinner, or gather around for a lavish family feast in our beautifully appointed dining room. The chef will take care of all your culinary needs, so you can focus on enjoying the ultimate wine country experience.

After a day of wine tasting, unwind in the property's luxurious amenities like swimming pool, hot tub and sauna. Imagine soaking in the hot tub under the stars, or sweating out the toxins in the sauna before diving into the refreshing pool.

Book your stay with us, and treat yourself to an unforgettable wine country getaway. With our idyllic setting, world-class amenities, and exclusive access to the vineyard, our property offers a truly unique and irresistible vacation experience. Don't miss out on this opportunity to indulge in luxury, adventure, and tranquility, all in one place.

And

Escape to paradise at our luxurious oceanfront villa in Costa Rica! Our property offers a unique blend of elegance, tranquility, and adventure with its direct access to a secluded and private beach, where you can enjoy the warm tropical waters and white sandy beaches in a more intimate and exclusive environment.

Picture yourself sipping on a refreshing tropical drink while lounging on the beach, or feeling the cool breeze while taking a stroll on the beach. Or, you could even enjoy a romantic dinner while taking in the beautiful ocean views from the fully equipped outdoor kitchen.

But the property's luxury doesn't stop there! Our rooftop terrace with Jacuzzi offers a panoramic ocean view, perfect for watching the sunset, stargazing or simply relaxing while enjoying the warm Costa Rican weather.

Book your stay with us, and treat yourself to an unforgettable beach vacation. With our idyllic setting, world-class amenities, and exclusive access to the private beach, our property offers a truly unique and irresistible vacation experience. Don't miss out on this opportunity to indulge in luxury, adventure, and tranquility, all in one place. Our concierge service is always available for any need or desire, from booking restaurant reservations to arranging tours of the local area, including jungle hiking and mangrove kayak tours.

2.

CHOOSING THE RIGHT LOCATION FOR YOUR LUXURY VACATION RENTAL

When it comes to luxury vacation rental properties, location is everything! As a property owner, you have the advantage of being able to choose the perfect location for your property and make the most of its potential. In this chapter, we'll be discussing the importance of choosing the right location for your luxury vacation rental, and providing you with some key tips and strategies for making the most of your property's location.

Analyzing the Local Market Conditions and Trends

The first step in choosing the right location for your luxury vacation rental is to analyze the local market conditions and trends. This includes researching tourism, property values, and demand for luxury rentals in the area. By understanding the local market, you'll be able to identify key factors that will impact the property's appeal and profitability. Understanding the market trends can also help you identify your target audience, the high season of demand and different market segments.

You can start by researching local tourism data to understand the number of tourists visiting the area, and the types of activities they are interested in. This can give you an idea of the type of guests who are likely to be interested in your property and the things they are looking for in a vacation rental. For example, if your property is located in a coastal area, it's likely that beach-related activities such as swimming and water sports will be popular among guests.

You can also research property values in the area to get a sense of the local real estate market. Look at property prices, average occupancy rates, and other factors that may affect the property's profitability. This information can give you an idea of the competition in the area and what you can do to stand out.

Another important aspect of analyzing the local market is understanding the demand for luxury rentals in the area. Researching the number of luxury vacation rentals in the area, the occupancy rates, and the average daily rates, can give you an idea of what you can expect in terms of bookings and revenue. Additionally, it can help you understand what type of amenities and services guests are looking for in a luxury vacation rental.

Leveraging the Benefits of the Property's Location
Once you've analyzed the local market, the next step is to evaluate how the property's location can be used to attract

specific types of guests. Take some time to identify the location's unique selling points, and think about how you can highlight these in your marketing and promotions. For example, if your property is located in a historic area with significant cultural or architectural landmarks, you can capitalize on this by creating a unique experience for guests that involves guided tours or other activities that highlight the history and culture of the area.

Additionally, leveraging the property's location can also mean thinking about additional services that can be provided. For example, if your property is located on a beachfront, you'll want to highlight the property's proximity to the beach in your listing. Also, you may want to think about offering additional services such as providing beach umbrellas and sun loungers, or a beach shuttle service. These small touches can help to make the property stand out and provide guests with a more memorable experience.

Optimizing Accessibility and Amenities

The final step in choosing the right location for your luxury vacation rental is to optimize the property's accessibility and amenities. This includes assessing the property's proximity to airports, train stations, public transportation, and local attractions. Providing guests with easy access to transportation and popular tourist destinations can help to make the property more appealing. Additionally, think about how you can en-hance the guest's experience by providing access to amenities such as a gym, a spa, a private pool or a concierge service. These services can help to make the property stand out and provide guests with a more luxurious and convenient experience.

Another important aspect to consider is transportation ser-vices for guests. Offering airport transfer or car rental services can not only make the guest experience more convenient but also increase the appeal of the property.

By following these tips, you'll be able to choose the right loca-tion for your luxury vacation rental and make the most of your property's potential. Remember, location is key when it comes to luxury vacation rental properties, and by choosing the right location, you'll be able to attract the right guests, receive great reviews, and maximize your property's profitability. It's all about providing an experience that not only meets but exceed guests expectations, by providing a luxurious, convenient, and unforgettable experience.

Summary

In conclusion, when it comes to luxury vacation rental proper-ties, the location is very important. By understanding the local market, leveraging the benefits of the property's location and optimizing accessibility and amenities, you can make the most of your property's potential. This will help you attract the right guests, get good reviews, and make more money. Remember, it's all about providing a luxurious, convenient, and unforgettable experience to your guests!

Little known fact

One little-known fact about choosing the right location for your luxury vacation rental is that proximity to natural landmarks and outdoor activities can be just as important as proximity to major cities and tourist destinations. Properties located near popular hiking trails, national parks, or other natural attractions can be highly desirable for guests looking to enjoy outdoor activities during their stay. By highlighting these nearby natural landmarks in your marketing and promotions, you can attract a different type of guest who is interested in outdoor adventure and nature.

Real life example

A property owner has a luxury vacation rental in the mountains of Colorado. Instead of solely focusing on the proximity to a nearby city or ski resort, the owner decides to focus on the property's proximity to a popular national park and nearby hiking trails. The owner highlights the nearby park and hiking trails in their marketing materials and provides guests with detailed trail maps, as well as information on guided hikes led by a local guide. The property also provides amenities such as outdoor gear rental and a shuttle service to the trailhead. By highlighting the outdoor activities available in the area, the owner is able to attract a different type of guest who is looking for a unique outdoor adventure experience.

Another real life example

A property owner has a luxury villa in Tuscany, Italy. Instead of only emphasizing the property's location in the heart of Tuscany, the owner decides to focus on the villa's proximity to renowned wine country. The owner promotes the villa as an ideal location for wine enthusiasts, they provides guests with curated wine-tasting experiences at nearby vineyards, and also create a wine-pairing menu with local wines. Additionally, the owner also offers cooking classes with local chefs that highlights the use of local and seasonal ingredients. The property also offers a complimentary bike rental to explore the surrounding countryside. By highlighting the region's rich culinary and wine culture in its offerings, the owner is able to attract a different type of guest who is interested in food and wine.

The description we would make

Escape to our luxury mountain retreat, nestled in the heart of Colorado's natural wonderland. Our property boasts breathtaking views and direct access to the area's top hiking trails, including the famous national park just steps away. Enjoy guided hikes led by a local expert, and make use of our complimentary outdoor gear rental and shuttle service to the trailhead. With all this outdoor adventure and natural beauty, our villa is perfect for the nature lover looking for an unforgettable escape.

and

Indulge in the Tuscan dream at our luxury villa, nestled in the heart of Tuscany's famous wine country. Sample local wines at nearby vineyards and dine on delicious Tuscan cuisine prepared with locally-sourced ingredients, all curated by us. Our villa also offers cooking classes with local chefs. With complimentary bike rental, explore the picturesque countryside, taste the wines and discover hidden gems of the region. Our villa offers the perfect blend of luxury, culture, and gastronomy for the discerning traveler.

3.

BUILDING AND DESIGNING THE PERFECT LUXURY VACATION RENTAL

Creating a luxury vacation rental property is more than just buying a beautiful property and putting it on the market. To truly stand out in the competitive luxury rental market, you need to design and build a space that not only looks and feels luxurious, but also caters to the needs and wants of your target market. In this chapter, we'll be discussing the key considerations and strategies for building and designing the perfect luxury vacation rental, even if you have already purchased a property and need to work with what you have.

Defining the Target Market's Needs and Wants

The first step in building and designing the perfect luxury vacation rental is to define the target market's needs and wants. This includes understanding the demographics of the guests you want to attract, their travel preferences, and the type of experience they are looking for. By understanding your target market, you'll be able to design and build a space that caters to their specific needs and wants.

For example, if your target market is families, you'll want to design and build a space that has enough room for everyone and provides amenities such as a pool and a playground. If your target market is business travelers, you'll want to design and build a space that has a dedicated workspace and high-speed internet.

Leveraging the Property's Features and Location

If you have already purchased a property, it's important to leverage the benefits of your property's features and location. Take advantage of the natural features, such as an ocean view, a lake or a beautiful garden, etc.. And if the property is located in an area with a strong tourist industry, such as near a popular tourist destination, take advantage of that as well. Use these features to create a unique experience for your guests, and make it clear in your marketing and promotions.

Creating a Luxurious Ambiance

Creating a luxurious ambiance is key to building and designing the perfect luxury vacation rental. This includes paying attention to the details and using high-end materials and finishes to create a sense of luxury and sophistication. Additionally, consider the type of lightening, textures, and the layout of the space, all of these elements can enhance the overall ambiance and atmosphere of the property.

Incorporating Modern Amenities

Incorporating modern amenities is essential in building and designing the perfect luxury vacation rental. This includes providing guests with high-speed internet, smart home technology, and other modern conveniences that are expected in a luxury rental. Additionally, think about incorporating extra touches such as a private pool, a spa, or a fitness center to provide guests with an added level of luxury and comfort.

Maximizing the Property's Potential

Finally, when building and designing the perfect luxury vacation rental, it's important to maximize the property's potential. This includes identifying areas of the property that could be utilized more effectively, or finding ways to add additional revenue streams, such as offering concierge services or organizing events on the property. By maximizing the property's potential, you'll be able to increase its earning potential and provide an even better experience for your guests.

In conclusion, building and designing the perfect luxury vacation rental is an important aspect of making a successful luxury vacation rental property. By understanding your target market, leveraging the property's features and location, creating a luxurious ambiance, incorporating modern amenities, and maximizing the property's potential, you'll be able to create a property that truly stands out in the market and appeals to your target guests. By focusing on these key elements, you'll be able to increase your earning potential, provide an unforgetta-ble experience for your guests, and ultimately achieve the goal of being a successful luxury vacation rental property owner.

Little known fact

A little-known fact about building and designing the perfect lux-ury vacation rental is the importance of using sustainable practices and incorporating eco-friendly elements. This not only helps to reduce the property's environmental impact, but it can also appeal to guests who are looking for sustainable and responsible travel options. Some of the ways that can be done is to install energy-efficient appliances, use non-toxic and natural materials, and to have an overall design of the property that is consistent with the local culture, such as by using local artisans and craftsman for furniture and decor. By implementing sustainable practices, a luxury vacation rental property can not only appeal to environmentally-conscious guests, but also save money on operating costs and position itself as a socially responsible business.

Real life example

A beachfront villa in the Caribbean has been designed and built with a focus on indoor-outdoor living and tropical ele-gance. The owners have used natural materials such as teak wood and bamboo to create a sense of warmth and harmony with the surrounding environment. The property boasts a large infinity pool with beautiful ocean views, and multiple outdoor living areas, perfect for entertaining and relaxing.

To maximize the property's potential, the owners have also incorporated modern amenities such as a gourmet kitchen, high-speed internet, and smart home technology. They also added a game room and a cinema room in the basement of the property to attract families and friends traveling together. Additionally, the property is staffed with a full-time concierge and a private chef, who can be hired to cook for guests during their stay, which adds an extra level of luxury and convenience for guests.

The property also has a private pier where guests can have boat excursions or rent a boat and sail along the Caribbean sea. This makes the property unique and gives a different perspective of the surrounding location.

Overall, the owners of this luxury vacation rental property have successfully created a luxurious ambiance and maximized the property's potential by focusing on natural materials, modern amenities, additional revenue streams, and unique experiences for guests.

A description that we would create for your vacation property

Escape to paradise in our luxurious beachfront villa. Enjoy indoor-outdoor living at its finest with breathtaking ocean views from your private infinity pool, multiple outdoor living areas and natural materials throughout the property that creates a sense of warmth and harmony with the surrounding environment. Fully staffed with a full-time concierge and a private chef, and equipped with modern amenities such as a gourmet kitchen, high-speed internet, and smart home technology, the property promises to make your Caribbean holiday unforgettable. And if you want something different you can have boat excursion or rent a boat to sail along the Caribbean sea, adding an extra level of luxury and convenience for guests.

4.

CAPTURING LIVELY AND EMOTION-EVOKING PHOTOS OF YOUR LUXURY VACATION RENTAL

Promoting and renting out a luxury vacation rental requires showcasing the property in the best light possible to attract potential guests and generate bookings. However, simply showcasing the property's features and amenities is not enough to stand out in today's highly competitive market. In order to capture potential guests' attention and create an emotional connection with them, it's essential to also create lively and visually striking photos that bring the emotion of wanting to be in that place now.

One way to create lively and visually striking photos is to take inspiration from Instagram, which is known for its visually-driven platform. To do this, use a combination of natural light, bold colors, and unique angles to create a sense of movement and energy in your photos. Additionally, consider incorporating elements such as people, pets, or activities to create a sense of life and activity in your photos.

Another important aspect is to focus on capturing the luxury and exclusivity of your property. This might include showcasing high-end finishes, luxurious furnishings, and upscale amenities. Use photos to create a sense of indulgence, pampering and relaxation. The key here is to showcase the vacation rental as a true escape, a place to get away from the daily routine and to indulge in luxury.

It's also important to take photos that showcase the property in different times of the day, this way you can give potential guests an idea of the different experiences they can have in the property, such as enjoying a sunrise or sunset by the pool, or having a romantic dinner in the terrace. In addition to that, taking some photos of the interior and exterior spaces during different seasons, and holidays could also create an emotional connection with the guests.

When taking photos, use a variety of angles and perspectives to give potential guests a complete understanding of the space. This might include wide-angle shots of the entire room, close-ups of unique features and amenities, and photos of outdoor spaces such as the pool, deck or terrace. Additionally, consider incorporating different photo formats, such as boomerangs, videos, and panoramas to create a sense of movement and energy.

Finally, as always, it's essential to hire a professional photographer. A professional photographer will have the experience, skills, and equipment to take photos that not only showcase the property's features and amenities but also the emotions that you want to convey. They will also have an understanding of Instagram's aesthetic and style, which will help you achieve that lively and visually striking look in your photos.

In summary, capturing lively and emotion-evoking photos of your luxury vacation rental is crucial for attracting potential guests and generating bookings. By taking inspiration from Instagram and using a combination of natural light, bold colors, and unique angles, showcasing luxury and exclusivity, capturing different times of the day, using a variety of angles and perspectives, incorporating different photo formats and hiring a professional photographer, you can create visually striking photos that evoke an emotional connection with potential guests and make them want to be in that place right now.

5.

ESTABLISHING A PRICING AND BOOKING STRATEGY

When it comes to renting your luxury vacation property, one of the most important aspects to consider is pricing and booking strategy. This is how you will establish how much to charge for your property, when to charge more or less, and how to make sure you are filling your calendar with the right guests. In this chapter, we will discuss the key considerations and strategies for pricing and booking your luxury vacation rental property.

Researching the Market and Setting Competitive Rates

The first step in establishing a pricing and booking strategy is researching the market and setting competitive rates. This includes researching the rates of similar properties in the area, as well as considering factors such as the season, occupancy levels, and any special events that may impact demand. By understanding the market, you will be able to set rates that are competitive and attractive to potential guests.

Utilizing Dynamic Pricing

To maximize your earning potential, you should also consider utilizing dynamic pricing. This is a strategy where you adjust your rates based on demand, with the goal of filling your calendar and maximizing your revenue. For example, you can charge higher rates during peak season and lower rates during shoulder season. You can also use tools that help you to adjust the prices based on the occupancy rate, and the day of the week.

Offering Special Deals and Discounts

Another way to fill your calendar and attract potential guests is by offering special deals and discounts. This can include things like last-minute deals, early bird discounts, and long-term stay discounts. Additionally, you can consider offering add-ons and packages, such as a concierge service or private chef, to further enhance the guest experience and increase your revenue.

Utilizing Online Travel Agents

Online Travel Agents (OTA) such as Airbnb, VRBO, and Booking.com can be a great way to increase the visibility of your property and reach a wider audience. By listing your property on these platforms, you'll be able to tap into their extensive customer base, and reach potential guests you may not have been able to otherwise. However, be aware that by listing your property on these platforms you'll have to pay a commission fee for each booking.

Creating a Strong Marketing and Promotion Strategy

Finally, it's important to create a strong marketing and promotion strategy to help fill your calendar. This includes utilizing social media, email marketing, and other digital marketing channels to promote your property and reach potential guests. Additionally, create a website of your own, and make sure it is professional and user-friendly, to showcase your property and provide potential guests with a seamless booking experience.

In conclusion, establishing a pricing and booking strategy is an essential aspect of making a successful luxury vacation rental.

Step-by-step guide

Step 1: Research the Market

- Use tools such as AirDNA, to analyze comparable properties in your area to determine an appropriate base rate for your property
- Factor in additional considerations such as the season, occupancy levels, and special events happening in the area
- Research demand and occupancy rates for different times of the year and week to understand when to adjust your pricing

Step 2: Utilize Dynamic Pricing

- Use dynamic pricing tools such as Beyond Pricing, PriceLabs to adjust your rates based on demand

- Increase rates during peak seasons and decrease rates during shoulder seasons
- Consider adjusting rates based on the day of the week

Step 3: Offer Special Deals and Discounts
- Use tools such as Rentals United or Kigo to create special deals, packages, and discounts
- Use tools like Reservation Key or Bókun to create packages, such as concierge service or spa treatments, to increase revenue
- Research and align your strategy with events and holidays happening in your area

Step 4: Utilize Online Travel Agents (OTA)
- List your property on popular OTA websites such as Airbnb, VRBO, and Booking.com
- Optimize your listings with professional pictures and detailed descriptions to stand out from the competition
- Be aware of the fees and commissions of OTA

Step 5: Develop a Strong Marketing and Promotion Strategy
- Use website builders like Wix or Squarespace to create a website for your property that is professional and user-friendly
- Use social media and email marketing tools such as MailChimp or Constant Contact to reach potential guests
- Respond promptly to inquiries and bookings

Step 6: Review and refine your strategy

- Use tools like Hostfully or OwnerRez to monitor the occupancy and revenue for your property
- Continuously review and adjust your pricing and booking strategy to optimize your revenue
- Be open to the feedback of your guests and try to meet their needs using tools such as GuestRevu or TrustYou

By following this step-by-step guide, you will be able to establish a pricing and booking strategy that is tailored to your specific property and local market conditions, with the goal of maximizing your revenue, filling your calendar with the right guests and providing an excellent experience for your guests.

Keep in mind that there are many different tools and companies available to help you establish your pricing and booking strategy, so it is important to do your research and find the ones that best meet your needs. Also, these tools and companies are subject to change and to have many alternatives, so it is important to keep looking for the best options that can help you with your property management. Additionally, it is important to remember that establishing a pricing and booking strategy is an ongoing process that requires continuous monitoring, adjustment and refinement, so you should be prepared to adapt your strategy as necessary and continue to improve your property management practices.

6.

MARKETING AND ADVERTISING YOUR LUXURY VACATION RENTAL

Marketing and advertising your luxury vacation rental property is crucial to ensure that it is seen by the right audience and effectively fills your calendar with bookings. Whether you are just starting out or have been in the business for a while, it's important to continuously evaluate and adjust your marketing and advertising strategies to ensure they are reaching the right audience and generating the best results.

One of the first steps in marketing and advertising your luxury vacation rental is developing a brand identity. This includes creating a unique and memorable name, logo and overall aesthetic that reflects the property's personality and setting. Consistency is key, so it is important to use this branding across all platforms, including your website, social media, and printed materials.

Social media platforms such as Facebook, Instagram, and Twitter are powerful tools to reach a wide audience and connect with potential guests. It's important to use high-quality images and videos to showcase your property and provide a sense of what guests can expect. Share relevant information about your property and the local area, such as upcoming events and activities. And make sure to interact with your followers, responding to comments and messages in a timely manner.

Having a website is a must-have, as it is often the first point of contact for potential guests. Make sure your website is professional and user-friendly, with clear navigation and easy-to-find information. Optimizing your website for search engines will increase visibility and make it easy for potential guests to find your property.

Utilizing Online Travel Agents (OTA) such as Airbnb, VRBO, and Booking.com can significantly increase your property's visibility and reach a wider audience. Make sure to optimize your listings with professional pictures, detailed descriptions, and pricing strategies that stand out from the competition.

Email marketing can be a powerful tool to reach potential guests. Create a mailing list of potential guests, past guests, and inquiries, and send them regular updates and special offers. Personalize your emails and make sure that they are visually appealing and easy to read.

Print advertising can be a great way to reach guests who prefer traditional methods of communication. Consider advertising your property in local newspapers, magazines, or in targeted advertising materials such as brochures or postcards.

Referral marketing can also be an effective way to promote your property. Encourage your current guests to refer friends and family to your property by offering incentives such as discounts or credit towards future stays. Ask for reviews and testimonials, and use these to further promote your property.

Paid advertising such as Google AdWords or Facebook Ads can reach a wider audience and increase visibility. Target your ads to your specific demographic, such as people searching for luxury vacation rentals in a specific location.

Lastly, it is important to continuously evaluate and adjust your marketing and advertising strategies to ensure they are reaching the right audience and generating the best results. Use tracking and analytics tools such as Google Analytics or SEMrush to monitor website traffic, social media engagement, and conversion rates. Make adjustments as necessary to optimize your marketing and advertising efforts.

In conclusion, having a solid marketing and advertising strategy in place is essential for your luxury vacation rental business. By building a brand identity, utilizing social media platforms, creating a professional website, utilizing online travel agents, email marketing, print advertising, referral marketing, paid advertising, and continuously evaluating and adjusting your strategy, you will be able to reach the right audience, fill your calendar with bookings, and ultimately increase your revenue. Remember to always be creative and willing to try new things in order to reach your audience, and to be responsive to guests' feedback.

Step-by-step guide

Step 1: Develop a Brand Identity

- Come up with a unique and memorable name, logo and overall aesthetic that reflects the property's personality and setting.
- Create a consistent branding across all platforms, including your website, social media, and printed materials.
- Consider hiring a branding agency like BrandHive or Lush Digital to help you develop your brand identity.

Step 2: Utilize Social Media

- Create accounts on popular social media platforms such as Facebook, Instagram, and Twitter.
- Share high-quality images and videos to showcase your property and provide a sense of what guests can expect.
- Share relevant information about your property and the local area, such as upcoming events and activities.
- Use a scheduling tool like Hootsuite or Buffer to schedule and automate your posts.

Step 3: Create a Professional Website

- Create a website that is professional and user-friendly, with clear navigation and easy-to-find information.
- Optimize your website for search engines using tools like Yoast or Ahrefs.
- Use a website builder like Wix or Squarespace to easily create a website.

Step 4: Utilize Online Travel Agents (OTA)

- Create listings on popular OTAs such as Airbnb, VRBO, and Booking.com.
- Optimize your listings with professional pictures, detailed descriptions, and pricing strategies that stand out from the competition.
- Use a pricing tool like BeyondPricing or PriceLabs to optimize your pricing strategy.

Step 5: Email Marketing

- Create a mailing list of potential guests, past guests, and inquiries.
- Send regular updates and special offers to your mailing list.
- Use an email marketing tool like Mailchimp or Constant Contact to manage and automate your email marketing campaigns.

Step 6: Print Advertising

- Consider advertising your property in local newspapers, magazines, or in targeted advertising materials such as brochures or postcards.
- Use a printing company like Vistaprint or Moo to print your advertising materials.

Step 7: Referral Marketing

- Encourage your current guests to refer friends and family to your property by offering incentives such as discounts or credit towards future stays.
- Ask for reviews and testimonials, and use these to further promote your property.

Step 8: Paid Advertising

- Invest in paid advertising such as Google AdWords or Facebook Ads to reach a wider audience and increase visibility.
- Use targeting options to reach specific demographics, such as people searching for luxury vacation rentals in a specific location.
- Use analytics and tracking tools like Google Analytics or SEMrush to monitor website traffic, social media engagement, and conversion rates.
- Make adjustments as necessary to optimize your marketing and advertising efforts.

By following this step-by-step guide and utilizing the tools and companies mentioned, you will be able to effectively market and advertise your luxury vacation rental to the right audience, fill your calendar with bookings, and ultimately increase your revenue.

7.

CREATING AN EXCEPTIONAL GUEST EXPERIENCE

Creating an exceptional guest experience is crucial for the success of your luxury vacation rental business. Not only will it lead to positive reviews, word-of-mouth referrals and repeat business, but it can also set you apart from your competitors.

First and foremost, it's important to be responsive to your guests' needs and address any issues they may have in a timely and professional manner. This can be done by providing clear and detailed instructions on how to access the property, how to operate any appliances or amenities, and where to find important information. Additionally, providing guests with a detailed guide to the local area, including recommended restaurants, activities and local events, is a great way to ensure they have a great time while they stay with you.

Make sure that your property is always clean and well-maintained. A clean and inviting space is essential to creating a positive first impression. You can hire a professional cleaning service or do it yourself, but make sure that the property is spotless before every guest arrival. Additionally, be sure to provide guests with the necessary amenities such as fresh linens, towels, and toiletries.

Another way to create an exceptional guest experience is by adding those little touches that make a big difference. This could include small gifts or treats left for guests on arrival, or a welcome note or gift basket. It could also include providing small items such as umbrellas or beach towels, which can make a guest's stay more comfortable.

Consider providing additional services such as private chefs, in-house spa treatments, or airport transportation. These added services can really set your property apart and create a truly luxurious experience for guests. Additionally, if you have a property management company, they can also offer additional services such as daily housekeeping, laundry and concierge services to your guests.

Providing guests with the latest technology is another way to create an exceptional guest experience. This could include things like high-speed internet, smart TV's, and streaming services, as well as other smart home technology such as keyless entry, thermostat control, and lighting control.

Lastly, It is important to keep in mind the importance of being environmentally friendly and socially responsible. You can promote this by providing guests with reusable containers, using energy-efficient appliances and LED lighting, using sustainable linens, and supporting local communities and businesses.

Creating an exceptional guest experience is about going above and beyond to meet and exceed guest expectations. It's about paying attention to the details and providing guests with the little touches that make their stay memorable. By providing a clean, well-maintained property, responsive customer service, additional services and amenities, and the latest technology, you can create a truly luxurious experience that will set your property apart from the competition. Additionally, by being environmentally friendly and socially responsible, you will also appeal to a growing segment of socially conscious travelers. By following these tips, you can create a guest experience that will lead to positive reviews, repeat business and ultimately increase your revenue.

Little-known fact

One little-known fact about creating an exceptional guest experience is that personalized touches can have a big impact. For example, providing guests with a customized welcome packet with local recommendations tailored to their interests and preferences, or even remembering a guest's name and preferences from a previous stay, can make them feel special and valued, leaving a lasting impression on them. Also, little gestures like providing complimentary water bottles, snacks, or even small gift can be a nice surprise that guests do not expect and they will appreciate. These small gestures will help you stand out and make it more likely that they will choose to stay with you again or recommend your property to friends and family.

Real life example

A couple had booked a weeklong stay at a luxury villa on the beach. From the moment they arrived, they were impressed with the property. It was beautifully decorated, clean and well-maintained, with stunning views of the ocean. But it was the little touches that truly made their stay exceptional.

Upon arrival, they were greeted with a welcome basket filled with local snacks and a handwritten note from the property owner. They were also provided with a detailed guide to the local area, including recommendations for restaurants, activities, and local events. The villa was equipped with the latest technology, including high-speed internet, smart TVs, and streaming services.

Throughout their stay, the guests were impressed with the level of service provided. The property management company was available 24/7 to address any issues or answer any questions they had. They also provided daily housekeeping services and complimentary laundry service. One evening, the guests were surprised with a private chef who cooked a delicious dinner for them on the terrace overlooking the ocean.

The couple was also pleased to see that the property was environmentally friendly and socially responsible. It was equipped with energy-efficient appliances and LED lighting, and used sustainable linens. Additionally, the property management company supported local communities and businesses.

Overall, the couple was truly amazed by the experience provided to them. They felt pampered and well taken care of throughout their stay, and the little touches made it feel like a truly luxury vacation. They couldn't wait to come back and tell their friends and family about their wonderful experience.

8.

MANAGING AND MAINTAINING YOUR LUXURY VACATION RENTAL

Managing and maintaining a luxury vacation rental can be a challenging task, but with the right approach, it can be a rewarding and profitable business. It's important to understand that this is not a passive investment, but a hands-on venture that requires your attention and dedication to succeed.

First, it's essential to have a proper management plan in place. This includes regular inspections of the property, scheduling routine maintenance and repairs, and keeping accurate records of all expenses. It's also important to establish clear policies and procedures for guests, such as check-in and check-out times, security deposits, and any other relevant information. Having a detailed manual that guests can refer to will make it easier for them to understand what is expected of them and reduce any confusion or misunderstandings.

It's also important to have a good team in place to assist with managing and maintaining the property. This can include a property manager, a cleaner, a handyman or repair person, and a bookkeeper or accountant. Having a team of professionals that you can rely on will make it easier to manage the property and provide guests with the level of service they expect.

When it comes to maintaining the property, it's important to keep up with routine cleaning, laundry, and general upkeep. This includes things like replacing light bulbs, replacing filters, and ensuring that appliances are in working order. It's also important to regularly inspect the property for any signs of wear and tear and make repairs as necessary. Additionally, providing guests with necessary amenities like fresh linens, towels, and toiletries is a must.

Another key element to managing and maintaining your luxury vacation rental is to stay current with the latest trends and technologies. This includes things like smart home technology, energy-efficient appliances, and sustainable materials. Being ahead of the curve will make your property more appealing to guests, and it will help you stay competitive in the marketplace.

Finally, you should consider investing in a comprehensive insurance policy to protect yourself and your guests from potential risks. This includes liability insurance, property insurance, and any additional coverage that may be required, such as workers' compensation insurance for employees.

Managing and maintaining a luxury vacation rental can be a lot of work, but with the right approach, it can be a fulfilling and profitable business. By having a proper management plan in place, establishing clear policies and procedures, and having a good team in place, you can ensure that your property is always in top condition and that guests have a wonderful experience. By staying current with the latest trends and technologies and investing in comprehensive insurance, you can protect yourself and your guests while also keeping your property competitive in the marketplace.

Step-by-step plan

Step 1: Develop a management plan

This includes setting clear policies and procedures for guests, scheduling regular inspections of the property, and keeping accurate records of all expenses.

Step 2: Assemble a team

This includes hiring a property manager, a cleaner, a handyman, and a bookkeeper or accountant. Make sure they are knowledgeable, dependable and can follow your procedures.

Step 3: Schedule regular maintenance and repairs

This includes routine cleaning, laundry, general upkeep, and making repairs as needed. This will ensure that the property is always in top condition for guests.

Step 4: Stay current with the latest trends and technologies

This includes using smart home technology, energy-efficient appliances, and sustainable materials. This will help make the property more appealing to guests and keep it competitive in the marketplace.

Step 5: Invest in insurance

Purchase a comprehensive insurance policy to protect yourself, your guests, and your property from potential risks.

Step 6: Regular Inspections

Do regular inspections of the property, both before guests arrive and after they leave. This will help you spot any issues early and make sure the property is always in good condition.

Step 7: Communication with Guests

Make sure to have good communication with guests, provide them with clear instructions and information, and be available to assist with any issues or concerns they may have.

Step 8: Guest Feedback

Encourage guests to provide feedback on their stay, this will allow you to see what they liked and what they didn't, and make improvements accordingly.

Step 9: Data Management

Keep track of your bookings, revenue, expenses and other data that will help you plan ahead and also make better decisions.

By following this step-by-step plan, you will be able to effectively manage and maintain your luxury vacation rental and ensure that guests have a memorable and enjoyable experience. You will also be able to maximize profitability and minimize any potential risks.

9.

USING TECHNOLOGY TO AUTOMATE YOUR LUXURY VACATION RENTAL

Technology has changed the way vacation rentals are managed, and it's essential to take advantage of the tools available to automate as many tasks as possible. One of the most important tools for managing your luxury vacation rental is a Property Management System (PMS).

A PMS is a software platform that helps manage everything from bookings and reservations to guest communications and payments. It allows you to easily manage your calendar, pricing, and availability, as well as create automated email and text messages to guests. Some PMS also provide integrations with key partners like Airbnb, Booking.com, and others which will allow you to manage all your listings in one platform.

One of the biggest benefits of using a PMS is the ability to automate repetitive tasks, such as sending out reservation confirmations, cancellation policies, and check-in instructions. This not only saves time but also ensures that guests have all the information they need, which can reduce confusion and complaints.

Another advantage of a PMS is the ability to set up automated pricing and availability based on demand. This will allow you to adjust rates according to peak and off-peak seasons, holidays, and special events. You will also be able to quickly update your availability calendar so that guests can book their stay with ease.

A PMS also allows you to easily track and manage payments, providing you with real-time data on revenue, occupancy, and other financials. This can help you make more informed decisions about pricing and availability.

Finally, a PMS can help you improve communication with guests by providing a central location for them to access information and communicate with you. Guest can also rate and review their stay which will help you improve your service over time.

By using a PMS, you can automate many tasks associated with managing a luxury vacation rental, which will free up time for more important things such as guest engagement, marketing and revenue management. This will make your rental business more efficient and profitable.

When choosing a PMS for your luxury vacation rental, it's important to consider the features that are most important to you, such as automation capabilities, pricing and availability management, and integrations with other platforms. It's also important to consider the cost and ease of use, so you can find a system that fits your budget and is easy to navigate.

Here is a list of key features and capabilities that a Property Management System (PMS) can offer for managing a luxury vacation rental:

- Calendar Management: Allows you to easily manage your calendar and availability, block off dates for maintenance or personal use, and set different pricing for peak and off-peak seasons.
- Channel Management: Integrate with popular booking platforms such as Airbnb, Booking.com, and others to manage all your listings from one place, and synchronize your availability and pricing across all channels.
- Reservation and Booking Management: Allows you to easily manage reservations and bookings, including the ability to accept payments, set up automated confirmation emails, and handle cancellations and refunds.
- Guest Management: Allows you to store guest information, communicate with guests before and during

their stay, manage guest reviews and ratings, and create targeted marketing campaigns.

- Financial Management: Provides real-time data on revenue, occupancy, and other financials, as well as the ability to set up automated billing and invoicing.
- Maintenance and Housekeeping Management: schedule and track maintenance tasks, manage cleaning schedule and inventory of supplies
- Automation: Automates repetitive tasks such as sending out confirmation emails, setting up cancellation policies, and sending out check-in instructions.
- Reporting: Provides detailed reports on occupancy, revenue, and other metrics that can help you make more informed decisions about pricing, availability, and marketing.
- Access Control: Control access to the PMS by creating roles and permissions for team members and partners.
- Mobile App Access: Most of PMS provide mobile app to access and manage your property on the go

Keep in mind that different PMS have different feature sets and capabilities, so it's important to research and compare different options before choosing one that meets your specific needs.

10.

BUILDING A SUSTAINABLE BUSINESS MODEL FOR LONG-TERM SUCCESS

Running a luxury vacation rental business can be a rewarding and profitable endeavor, but it's important to have a sustainable business model in place to ensure long-term success. A sustainable business model is one that generates enough revenue to cover expenses and provide a reasonable return on investment, while also being responsive to changing market conditions and consumer preferences.

One of the key components of a sustainable business model is pricing strategy. Pricing your rental correctly is essential to attract the right type of guests, while also generating enough revenue to cover your expenses and provide a return on investment. It's important to research the local market and set prices that are competitive, while also taking into account your property's unique features and amenities. Pricing can be flexible, changing according to demand and seasonality.

Another important aspect of a sustainable business model is cost management. It's important to keep operating costs low, without sacrificing the guest experience. This can include outsourcing certain tasks, such as cleaning and maintenance, using energy-efficient appliances, and implementing recycling and waste reduction programs.

Marketing and advertising are also key to building a sustainable business model. By understanding your target market and identifying their preferences and needs, you can create effective marketing campaigns that will drive bookings and revenue. Utilizing different channels such as social media, SEO and paid ads can be very effective in reaching a large audience.

In addition to pricing, cost management, and marketing, another crucial aspect of a sustainable business model is guest satisfaction and experience. A positive guest experience can lead to positive reviews, increased bookings, and a loyal customer base. This can be achieved by investing in top-notch amenities, providing excellent customer service, and being responsive to guests' needs and concerns.

Finally, keeping a keen eye on performance indicators, such as occupancy rate, revenue per booking and cost of acquisition, can help you make informed business decisions, and adapt to changing market conditions.

In summary, building a sustainable business model for your luxury vacation rental requires a combination of effective pricing strategy, cost management, marketing, guest satisfaction and ongoing performance monitoring. By focusing on these key areas, you can create a business that generates consistent revenue and long-term success.

11 QUESTIONS TO ASK YOURSELF BEFORE CHOOSING A VACATION RENTAL MANAGEMENT COMPANY

You've been managing your vacation rental property for a while, but now you're considering handing over the responsibility to a professional management company. It's a wise decision, as time and peace of mind are priceless! However, with so many management companies out there, how do you choose the best one that meets your specific needs? In this chapter, we'll guide you through the process by providing 11 essential questions to ask during your selection interviews.

1. What is your strategy for increasing my rental income? A good management company should have a clear strategy for maximizing your rental income. Look for companies that use data-driven approaches like dynamic pricing systems to determine optimal rates and occupancy. A serious management company should also focus on reducing expenses and optimizing the occupancy rate to protect your assets.

2. What is your recipe for success in providing an unforgettable guest experience? An exceptional guest experience is crucial for repeat bookings and positive reviews. Inquire about the management company's

approach to creating memorable guest experiences. Words, photos, and positive feedback play a significant role, so ask how they will utilize these to enhance your property's appeal.

3. What is included in your management fee? Management fees can vary widely based on the services offered. Evaluate the fee in relation to the services provided and their impact on your overall income. Consider the revenue optimization strategy as well; a lower or higher management fee may not guarantee optimal income. Request an analysis of profitability potential based on comparables.

4. What are your packages? Different management companies offer various packages. Determine your specific needs and look for a company that can accommodate them. Some offer a one-size-fits-all approach, while others provide more flexibility with tailored packages.

5. How do you protect my assets and ensure guest satisfaction? A reliable management company should have a strategy for filtering out undesirable guests and handling potential issues to protect your property and your reputation. Ask about their screening process and how they handle guest complaints or breakages.

6. What is your target occupancy rate? Be cautious of companies that promise unusually high occupancy rates. Look for a company that aims for the "sweet spot," balancing occupancy and income to ensure you

have enough personal time with your property while maximizing revenue.

7. On which platforms will you market my property? A successful marketing strategy involves promoting your property on multiple platforms, not just relying on one. Look for a company that will showcase your property on various global and local platforms and leverage social media for maximum exposure.

8. How do you ensure quality control? Cleanliness and maintenance are critical factors in guest satisfaction. Inquire about the management company's approach to housekeeping, property maintenance, and overall quality control to maintain positive reviews.

9. How do you handle emergency situations? Prompt response and action in emergency situations are vital for guest satisfaction. Ask how the management company handles emergencies and ensures quick and efficient service.

10. How can I use my property? A good company should provide you with a self-service portal where you can make your own reservations and view the property's past and future booking calendar. Additionally, does this company limit you in your private bookings? Reserver.ca does not impose any restrictions on its partners regarding private bookings.

11. What do you have planned to save me time and automate tasks? Time-saving solutions can significantly impact your efficiency as a property owner. Inquire

about automation tools and systems the management company uses to streamline repetitive tasks and improve your overall experience.

In conclusion, entrusting the management of your vacation rental property to a specialized company can save you time, money, and hassle. By asking these 11 essential questions, you'll be well-equipped to find the right management company that aligns with your goals and ensures the success of your vacation rental business.

At Reserver.ca we've already answered all those questions and have experience proof in hand.

Upgrade your luxury property's earning potential and ensure a seamless rental experience with the help of our expert team. Our tailored solutions cater to your specific needs, whether you're seeking a one-time consultation or a full-service solution. Don't miss out the chance to become a partner of us on maximizing your property's earning potential and providing guests with an unforgettable experience.

Contact us now at 1 (833) 335-2583 or partnerup@reserver.ca to elevate your rental game to the next level. Plus, take advantage of our exclusive offer - a FREE analysis of your property's rental potential. Let us show you how we can help you achieve unparalleled success in the vacation rental market! Don't wait, get in touch today and unlock the true potential of your luxury vacation rental.

ABOUT US

Patrick Poulin

A visionary entrepreneur in the real estate sector, focusing on the development, training, and coaching of professionals in the vacation chalet and short-term rental market. With a wealth of experience in property development and investment strategies, he has established himself as a leading authority in the industry. Patrick's venture into real estate commenced with the ownership of a charming chalet, igniting his passion for crafting exceptional guest experiences, and maximizing property profitability.

Through his pioneering endeavors at Immofacile, Patrick has introduced innovative approaches to creative financing and property management, setting a new benchmark for the industry. His appearances on various television programs have not only showcased his expertise but have also provided valuable insights into the complex dynamics of the real estate market. At Reserver.ca, he plays a key role in the Strategy and Finance department.

In 2018, Patrick Poulin teamed up with his esteemed business partner, Patrick Beland, to establish Reserver.ca, a dynamic property management company dedicated to delivering superior results for property investors. Patrick's strategic vision and deep understanding of real estate dynamics have been instrumental in propelling Reserver.ca to the forefront of the industry.

Patrick Beland

A prominent figure in real estate prospecting and rental yield optimization, Patrick Beland owns rental properties globally and has played a pivotal role in guiding clients toward maximizing their rental income and overall profitability. With over 25 years of extensive experience in the technology sector, he brings a unique perspective to the company. Patrick Beland's latest venture, BNBMatrix.com, is a cutting-edge business intelligence application tailored to the specific requirements of the short-term rental industry. The platform empowers property investors to make informed decisions by analyzing critical data and identifying the most lucrative investment opportunities in Quebec and beyond. In Reserver.ca, he spearheads the Technology and Marketing division.

Prior to Reserver.ca, both Patricks embarked on an ambitious project in the lively locale of Sainte-Adèle, one of the last remaining developments in the prime tourist area near Montreal.

This initiative laid the groundwork for an integrated development exclusively dedicated to short-term rentals, encompassing over 70 meticulously designed plots. The project stands as a testament to Patrick's visionary leadership and unwavering commitment to meeting the evolving demands of the market.

For further insights into the exceptional contributions of Patrick Poulin and Patrick Beland in the real estate sector, visit airbnbinvestmentproperty.com, a comprehensive resource highlighting their profound insights and accomplishments in the field.

Stephanie Bessette

A seasoned professional with an illustrious career spanning over two decades in the customer service industry, currently serves as the General Manager of Reserver.ca. Her unwavering commitment to ensuring seamless guest experiences and active involvement in the strategic development of the company have earned her the trust and appreciation of clients worldwide. Stephanie's dedication to excellence and her passion for delivering exceptional service reflect her deep-seated commitment to raising the standards of the hospitality industry. At Reserver.ca, she oversees the Operations and Human Resources pillar.

We are confident that our expertise and commitment to providing exceptional experiences to our clients make us the ideal choice to guide investors towards success. Join us today to give your vacation rental business an unparalleled competitive advantage!

WHAT OUR PARTNERS
THINK OF US

"Wow! I can't say enough about Reserver.ca's incredible team! They treated our vacation rental as if it were their own, ensuring everything went smoothly. Their quick response to guest inquiries and exceptional efficiency made our property a huge hit with travelers. Highly recommended!"

- Natalie Babin

"The Reserver.ca team is like magic! Our rental income sky-rocketed thanks to their brilliant pricing strategies and marketing skills. They attracted more travelers throughout the year, and we couldn't be happier with the results!"

- Jean-Luc Dion

"Our property has become an attraction thanks to Reserver.ca's photography and marketing skills. Their stunning listings and clever promotions attracted more bookings than we could have ever imagined!"

- Claude Chouinard

"Before and after Covid, the Reserver.ca team remained at the top of their expertise, even in times of highs and lows. Before the pandemic, their innovative approach reached new heights in vacation property management, with record rental income and satisfied guests. They made the most of every opportunity for our rentals, creating unforgettable experiences for our guests."

- Charles Lussier

"Trustworthy and transparent - that's the Reserver.ca team! I have complete confidence in their financial management. Their clear reports and efficiency reassure me. I know my investment is in good hands."

- Catherine Florent

"Reserver.ca offers a turnkey management service that truly impressed me. Their professional approach and attention to both tenants and property owners are highly appreciated. Thanks to them, I was able to manage my property with peace of mind. I highly recommend them to anyone looking for a competent team to manage their real estate assets. Best wishes to the entire Reserver.ca team!"

- David Aubry

"The team has been managing my condos at Suites-Sur-Lac for two years now, and I have nothing but praise. Communication, advertising, customer experience, and respect are just a few examples of the team's strengths at Reserver.ca. The Reserver.ca experience goes far beyond managing my units.

I have the privilege of having passionate, attentive, and innovative people by my side. Real estate investors who genuinely care about the success of their peers and are always open to sharing their past experiences. When you want to build a strong and competent network, you choose Reserver.ca."

- Patrick Gilbert

www.ingramcontent.com/pod-product-compliance
Lightning Source LLC
Chambersburg PA
CBHW072340290526
45794CB00002B/955